Stodgepodge!

Jeremy Strong

Illustrated by Giulia Orecchia

OXFORD
UNIVERSITY PRESS

Chapter 1

Stodgepodge!

'What is it?' asked Cleo. She stared grumpily at her breakfast bowl.

'Guess,' grunted Dad as he turned away from the table.

Cleo's little brother, Alfie, grinned at her cheekily. 'Go on, guess!' he said.

Cleo picked up her spoon and splatted the top of the grey-brown lump in her bowl.

'Is it a dead jellyfish?' she asked.

Alfie squeaked with laughter. 'No!' he said.

'Is it lots of snails' stomachs turned inside out?' Cleo asked.

'No!' yelled Alfie, almost falling off his chair. 'It's stodgepodge!'

CRASH!

Alfie *did* fall off his chair.

Stodgepodge. That's what Cleo and Alfie called their dad's porridge. Dad made the worst porridge in the world. No, that's wrong. Dad made the worst porridge in the *universe*! And now it was sitting in Cleo's breakfast bowl.

'Eat it up,' Dad growled.
'It's good for you.'

Chapter 2
Big jumps

Cleo headed for school with Alfie. They had escaped the nightmare porridge at last. That was because Cleo had stuck some of it under her chair when Dad wasn't looking. She had put the rest in Alfie's new trainers when *he* wasn't looking. Well, she had to hide it *somewhere*.

Cleo felt strangely light on the way to school. She was as bouncy as a ping-pong ball. Her long, dark hair floated behind her like wisps of silk.

When they reached school, everyone was racing around and leaping about like penguins on pogo sticks.

'I bet I can jump up and touch the top of the wall,' boasted Cleo's friend, Billy.

'I bet you can't!' Cleo dared him.

So Billy jumped, and he landed *on top* of the wall! It was twice as tall as he was. Wow!

Cleo jumped up and landed there too. She stared at Billy. It was weird. How could they make such big leaps? When they jumped down it felt as if they were gliding. This was fantastic – but strange.

The whistle went and they trooped into school. That was when things got even stranger.

Chapter 3

What's happening?

Mrs McNurdle, Cleo's teacher, was a large woman with a large nose. She was wearing a large smile, so everyone knew that she was in a good mood.

'I feel so bouncy today,' she told her class. 'Let's write some bouncy stories.'

Cleo went to her tray to get her workbook and pencil. The moment she pulled out the tray everything inside it began to float up into the air. Up went her pencil and eraser and ruler and workbook. Up went her maths book and a sock that she didn't even know was there.

In fact, right across the classroom, the same thing was happening. Every small object was starting to float upwards.

The children stared at the ceiling. It was covered with cardigans and shirts, swimming shorts, shoes, books, pencils, crayons, rulers and all sorts. In fact, they only just managed to stop the hamster's cage from floating up there too.

The children pointed at each other and burst out laughing. Everyone's hair was standing on end! They began shouting. What was going on?

Mrs McNurdle didn't know what to do. 'The world's going mad!' she cried. And as she got off her chair, it drifted up to the ceiling too! 'Come back!' she ordered.

Chapter 4

Big danger!

Meanwhile, the same thing was happening right across the country. The Prime Minister had to go on television to make a special announcement.

'Good afternoon,' he began. 'I am sure that all of you will have noticed that more and more things are floating up into the sky.'

As he said this, the Prime Minister himself began to drift upwards from his chair. Two men wearing big iron boots stomped across. They pulled the PM down and tied him to several large weights so he wouldn't float off again.

'A giant black hole is approaching our planet. The black hole is sucking up everything it can. This is very dangerous. Please stay indoors. Wear iron boots or tie yourself to something big and heavy. Animals like elephants and whales make excellent weights.'

'That man's a noodle-poodle,' muttered Mrs McNurdle. 'Where am I going to find an elephant?'

'Our scientists are working on a plan to save the world,' said the Prime Minister. 'Keep watching the news for more updates.'

Then the broadcast finished. Which was just as well, because suddenly the television floated up, drifted out of the window and disappeared into space.

Chapter 5

Bad news

Parents hurried to the school to collect their children and make sure they were safe. At least they *tried* to hurry, but they were all wearing iron boots so they didn't float away. Some parents tried driving their cars, but the cars had to be tied down with weights too.

Cleo and Alfie had to wear giant iron wellies to get home safely. By the time they got inside they found that everything in the house was bobbing against the ceiling. Luckily, Cleo and Alfie also floated up there once they took their wellies off, so they were able to eat their supper, even if it was upside down.

That night was the strangest night ever for Cleo and Alfie. Their parents had to turn the children's beds over so they could sleep upside down on the ceiling. They probably had upside down dreams too.

In the morning, they couldn't get up because they had to get *down* instead. In fact, they had to get dressed upside down on the ceiling, because everything was up *there* instead of being on the floor.

They watched the morning news on the television (which was stuck up by the ceiling too). The woman on the news looked very scared. She said that the world's scientists didn't know what to do. Suddenly, she started to shout.

'The black hole is getting closer. Soon everyone will be sucked up into it. Prepare to meet your doom. This is the end of the world! Help!'

The family sat on the upside down sofa and stared at each other in alarm.

Chapter 6

Cleo's brain explodes!

Cleo was puzzled. She suddenly remembered seeing Alfie's new trainers on the floor. In fact, everything was stuck to the ceiling except those shoes and one chair. She just could not understand why they weren't up there with everything else. That was when she remembered what was inside those trainers and under that chair. *Stodgepodge*!

Cleo's brain was whizzing and whirring with an extraordinary idea.

'Hey!' she cried. 'I bet if we filled the black hole with Dad's stodgepodge it would probably *burst* or something! It's the stickiest, stodgiest stuff in the universe!'

Mum looked at Dad. Dad looked at Mum. They both looked at Cleo and Alfie.

'Do you know? I think that might work!' cried Mum. 'Dad, you make as much of your porridge as you can. I must telephone the Prime Minister!'

The Prime Minister was very excited to hear about Dad's stodgepodge. He sent round a whole army of cooks to help Dad make as much of it as possible.

The stodgepodge was taken away in giant tankers and loaded on to rockets. The rockets were blasted into space and they headed straight for the black hole.

SPLONK!

Chapter 7

The secret weapon

One by one, the rockets fired stodgepodge into the black hole. The black hole gulped. It chewed and hiccuped and burped. It burped again, and then ...

KER-BOOOOM!

It shattered into one million and seventy-two pieces.

That was the end of the black hole.
Everything came floating back down again.
Stodgepodge had saved the world!

Cleo and her family were heroes.
They were given a special tea at the Prime
Minister's house. Not only that, but the
Prime Minister declared that stodgepodge
was definitely a secret weapon and *very*
dangerous. He said Dad was not allowed
to make it any more unless Earth was
threatened by another black hole.
Cleo was over the moon about
that, but not for long.

'I don't know
what you're
grinning about,
Cleo,' said Dad.

'You've ruined Alfie's new trainers. You'll have to buy him a new pair with your pocket money!'

'But it was *your* stodgepodge that ruined them!' Cleo shouted at Dad.

'I know it was!' Dad shouted back. 'But *you* put the stodgepodge in them!'

'Exactly!' Alfie squawked. 'I want new trainers!'

In fact, if you listen carefully, you can still hear them arguing over it now.

About the author

I was educated with a lot of shouting at schools in London and more quietly at York University. I spent several years teaching in primary schools until I tunnelled my way out with pen and paper. I have married and remarried, acquiring a son and daughter, two step-daughters, five grandchildren and three cats. My hobbies include eating different types of bread and sleeping. I live near Bath.

I've never really liked porridge, so writing a story about using it to save the world seemed like a good way to make myself feel better! Putting stodgepodge in Alfie's shoes was just the sort of thing my brothers and sister and I used to do to each other. We still do – and we're all grown up now!